DUCKS

FARM ANIMAL DISCOVERY LIBRARY

Lynn M. Stone

Rourke Corporation, Inc.
Vero Beach, Florida 32964

PHOTO CREDITS

All photos by the author

ACKNOWLEDGEMENTS

The author thanks the following for assistance in the
preparation of photos for this book: Dave Heffernan/
Blackberry Historical Farm Village, Aurora, Ill.; Marion Behling,
St. Charles, Ill.

LIBRARY OF CONGRESS
Library of Congress Cataloging-in-Publication Data
Stone, Lynn M.
  Ducks / by Lynn M. Stone.

    p. cm. — (Farm animal discovery library)
    Summary: Introduces the physical characteristics, habits,
and natural environment of ducks.
    ISBN 0-86593-037-6
    1. Ducks—Juvenile literature. [1. Ducks.] I. Title. II. Series:
Stone, Lynn M. Farm animal discovery library.
SF505.3.S76   1990
636.5'97—dc20   89-29985
                                 CIP
                                 AC

TABLE OF CONTENTS

DUCKS

Ducks are plump birds with stubby legs and broad, webbed feet. They are more at home in the water than on land.

Ducks that live on farms are slower and heavier than wild ducks.

Farm, or **domestic,** ducks stay in pens, pastures, coops, and barnyards.

Domestic ducks are raised for their meat, eggs, and feathers.

Ducks are related to geese and swans. Domestic geese are generally much heavier than ducks.

The first farm ducks were probably tamed in China over 2,000 years ago.

Embden goose

HOW DUCKS LOOK

In the United States, the most common domestic ducks are white Pekins. Both **drakes** (males) and **hens** (females) are white.

Muscovy ducks, also common on farms, may be white or a blend of dark colors. Muscovy drakes have a warty red knob on their bills.

Pekin ducks weigh about eight pounds. Some domestic ducks weigh up to 16 pounds.

A duck's feet are far apart. When a duck walks, its flat feet point inward. The duck waddles.

In the water, a duck is graceful.

*Mallard hen
and ducklings*

WHERE DUCKS LIVE

Small numbers of domestic ducks live on farms throughout North America. Many farms which have turkeys or chickens also have a few ducks.

Ducks are not nearly as popular a food in North America as turkeys and chickens are.

About three of every five domestic ducks raised in the United States live on Long Island, New York. Several big farms there specialize in ducks.

Children's zoos, garden parks, and people who raise **waterfowl** for show raise domestic ducks, too.

*Ducks have broad,
webbed feet*

BREEDS OF DUCKS

The different kinds of domestic ducks are called **breeds.** Breeds differ in size, color, shape, and other features.

All of the domestic duck breeds resulted from man's capture, long ago, of two kinds of wild ducks.

Most of the farm ducks in the United States began with wild mallard ducks *(Anas platyrhynchos).*

The snow-white Pekin ducks came from mallards.

Wild muscovy ducks *(Cairina moschata)* from South America also led to domestic breeds.

Domestic ducks can be up to three times larger than their wild ancestors.

Muscovy drake

Pekin duck

Muscovy ducklings

WILD DUCKS

Wild ducks live all over the world where they can find ponds, lakes, marshes, or sea coasts.

One of the world's most widespread ducks is the mallard, or "greenhead."

There are about 125 kinds of wild ducks. Mallards, for example, are one of the "dabbling" ducks. They dabble, or dip, their heads into water to feed. Sea ducks and pochards dive.

Muscovy ducks are, like wild North American wood ducks, "perching" ducks. They often perch on tree limbs.

Wild mallard drake

BABY DUCKS

A mother duck **incubates,** or warms, her five to twelve eggs for about a month before they hatch. Baby ducks, or **ducklings,** can leave the nest when they are about 24 hours old.

Like baby geese, swans, and chickens, ducks can walk and feed themselves within hours after hatching. Between five and eight weeks of age, a duck can fly.

Wild ducks can live several years. Most domestic ducks in the United States are sold for meat at eight weeks of age.

Duck's nest of down

HOW DUCKS ARE RAISED

Ducks snip greens with the rough edges of their bill and pluck insects from the grass. They also strain food from water and dabble for water plants.

On large duck farms, duck food is controlled by the farmers. Those ducks are fed a high-protein diet so they will weigh seven pounds in eight weeks. Then they are taken to market.

Most ducks are kept in fenced areas. They have huts or barns for shelter.

Pekin ducks

HOW DUCKS ACT

Most farmers make certain that their ducks have a pond or stream. Ducks float easily because their feathers are waterproof.

Ducks work hard to keep their feathers waterproof. A duck dips its bill into the oil its body makes, then pulls its feathers through its bill.

This is called **preening.** By preening, a duck keeps its feathers clean and waterproof. Water rolls off clean feathers.

Ducks also spend time resting with heads tucked against their backs.

Pekin ducks preening

HOW DUCKS ARE USED

Ducks in the United States are raised mainly for their meat. Duck meat is dark and contains more iron and fat than chicken or turkey.

Duck eggs are not a popular food in the United States, but they are commonly used in some other countries. Ducks are excellent egg layers. Campbell ducks average about one egg per day.

The fuzzy down feathers that make up a duck's "underwear" are valuable for pillows, jackets, and sleeping bags. Down lining is extremely warm.

Glossary

breed (BREED)—closely related group of animals that came about through man's help; a type of domestic duck

domestic (dum ES tik)—tamed and raised by man

drake (DRAKE)—male duck

duckling (DUCK ling)—a baby duck

hen (HEN)—a female duck or any of several other female birds

incubate (INK you bate)—to keep eggs warm until they hatch

preen (PREEN)—to carefully clean and oil feathers

waterfowl (WATER fowl)—the ducks, geese, and swans of the world

INDEX